# Contents

Words appearing in the text in bold, **like this**, are explained in the Glossary.

# Asteroids, comets, and meteoroids

We normally think of our **Solar System** as the Sun, the **planets**, and their **moons**. However, there are all sorts of other things to be discovered if you know where to look.

## Snowballs in space

One of the most impressive things to observe in the night sky is a bright **comet** with a long tail. Comets are like large, dirty snowballs with bits of rock in them. But they are much bigger than any snowball on Earth! They can be several kilometres across – more like icebergs floating through space. Occasionally a comet bright enough to see with the naked eye appears in the sky. However, you need binoculars or a telescope to see most comets.

The great comets are spectacular sights to see.

## SCIENCE FACT OR SCIENCE FICTION?

In the film *Armageddon*, there is an asteroid racing towards the Earth. Bruce Willis and his team go up in a Space Shuttle to save the Earth. They land on the asteroid and plant bombs on it. When the bombs explode, the asteroid breaks into pieces. This idea might work if an asteroid really was heading for Earth. However, many scientists think that although the asteroid would break up, the pieces would still hit the Earth.

Another type of Solar System object is an **asteroid**. Asteroids can be made of rock, metal or carbon, and ice. They are sometimes called planetoids or minor planets. Asteroids can be quite large – up to 1000 km (600 miles) across. To see an asteroid, you will need a good telescope, as they are usually a long way from Earth.

There are a lot of smaller things out there in the Solar System. **Meteoroids** are small chunks knocked off asteroids, planets, moons, or comets. There is even some dust left from the formation of the Solar System.

## Crash landings

You can see meteoroids as they crash into the Earth, creating streaks of light called **meteors** or shooting stars. Some bigger lumps of rock are not completely burned up in the **atmosphere**, but crash into the Earth's surface. They are called **meteorites**.

Meteorites land on the Earth every day, but what about comets and asteroids? There is evidence that they have crashed into the Earth, the Moon, and other planets in the past so it is likely to happen again. The question is, when?

Between Mars and Jupiter there is a region called the **asteroid belt**, containing billions of asteroids of all sizes.

# Asteroids or planets?

Asteroids are found all over the Solar System. They **orbit** around the Sun and are made of rock, stone, and ice. They come in all shapes and sizes. Most asteroids are very small, the size of small boulders. However, there are some much larger asteroids. The largest object in the asteroid belt is called Ceres. It is 933 km (580 miles) across. Ceres is so large that it is now called a "**dwarf planet**". There are also some large objects beyond the orbit of Neptune.

Asteroids are chunks of rock and metal, left over from the formation of the Solar System. They come in all sorts of interesting shapes.

## HOW IT WORKS:
### The long arm of the Sun

The Sun is huge and contains a lot of **matter**. This means that its gravitational pull is very strong and stretches out a long way into space. This gravitational pull keeps the asteroids orbiting the Sun. If an asteroid gets too close to a large planet, the **gravity** from that planet will also tug on the asteroid. This can change the asteroid's orbit and can even make the asteroid crash into the planet.

Like the planets, asteroids move around the Sun along a path called an orbit. The shape of this orbit is an **ellipse**, which is a squashed circle. Scientists don't just want to know that asteroids are there, they also want to know where they will be next. To do this they need to work out the exact orbit of the asteroid. They can use this to predict whether the asteroid will ever hit the Earth, or another planet or moon. Scientists have worked out the orbits for over 40,000 asteroids so far. The Infrared Space Observatory has estimated that there are between 1.1 million and 1.9 million asteroids larger than 1 km (0.6 mile) in the asteroid belt, so they have a lot more work to do.

This is an artist's impression of the asteroid that hit the Earth around 65 million years ago, possibly causing the extinction of the dinosaurs.

# Where are asteroids found?

Asteroids are divided into four different groups, depending on where they are found in the Solar System. These groups are the main belt asteroids, the Trojans, the Centaurs and the near-Earth asteroids.

## The main belt asteroids

The best-known asteroids are the main belt asteroids. These are found in the asteroid belt, between Mars and Jupiter. The belt contains about 1.5 million asteroids larger than 1 km (0.6 mile) across, as well as billions of smaller ones. The first asteroids discovered – Ceres, Pallas, Juno and Vesta – were all main belt asteroids.

## The Trojans

Trojan asteroids travel in a similar orbit as Jupiter. Some of them travel around the Sun about a sixth of an orbit ahead of Jupiter, while others follow the same distance behind. Astronomers think that these asteroids have probably been there since the Solar System was formed. Since they are moving around the Sun in a similar orbit to Jupiter, they are very unlikely to leave this and hit the Earth.

## BIOGRAPHY:
### Giuseppe Piazzi (1746–1826)

The Swiss astronomer Giuseppe Piazzi was the first person to discover an asteroid. On 1 January 1801 he discovered an object that seemed like a small planet. He named it Ceres after the Sicilian goddess of grain. It is the largest known asteroid in the main asteroid belt and is 933 km (580 miles) across.

Main belt asteroids

Trojans

Jupiter

Trojans

Saturn

Asteroids are found all over the Solar System. Some are found close to Earth and others are beyond the planet Neptune.

## The Centaurs

Between the orbits of Jupiter, Saturn, Uranus, and Neptune are the Centaur asteroids. These asteroids don't always stay in the same place. The gravity of the big planets, particularly Jupiter, can pull on them and change their orbits if the asteroids pass too close by. If the asteroids get really close to a planet, gravity can pull the asteroids in and make them orbit the planet. Some of the moons of the giant planets may once have been asteroids.

## Near-Earth asteroids

Finally, there are the near-Earth asteroids. These are asteroids dotted around the Solar System and they have orbits that bring them close to the orbit of the Earth. Scientists are keen to keep an eye on these asteroids, in case they get too close to the Earth and crash into it. Scientists have found over 790 near-Earth asteroids that are more than 1 km (0.6 mile) wide, but there may be many more of them.

# What is an asteroid made from?

Not all rocks on Earth are the same – there are many different types. In the same way, asteroids can be made from very different materials. Some asteroids are soft and crumbly, while others are hard and shiny. Some contain metals like iron and nickel.

Different materials reflect light in different ways. So scientists examine the way light is reflected from asteroids to find out what they are made from. There seem to be three main types: stony asteroids, metallic asteroids, and carbonaceous asteroids.

## Stony asteroids

Stony, or S-type asteroids, make up about 17 per cent of all asteroids. These asteroids are bright, because they reflect sunlight very well. Eros (see pages 14–15) is an example of a stony asteroid.

## Metallic asteroids

Metallic, or M-type asteroids, are made from nickel and iron, just like the **cores** of the planets and moons. Scientists think that these metallic asteroids are probably the remains of planets that did not finish forming. As you might expect, metal can reflect sunlight very well, so these asteroids are also bright. Only about 8 per cent of asteroids are metallic. Kleopatra is a metallic asteroid.

Kleopatra's unusual shape could be due to a collision with another asteroid.

**Deimos**

**Phobos**

Some asteroids get caught by a planet's gravity. Scientists think that Mars' moons used to be asteroids.

## HOT NEWS:

The asteroid Kleopatra was discovered in 1880, but in 2000 it became the first asteroid in the main asteroid belt to be imaged using **radar**. Astronomers used the Arecibo **radio telescope** in Puerto Rico to bounce signals off Kleopatra. The asteroid was 171 million km (106 million miles) from Earth at the time. Kleopatra is 217 km (135 miles) long and 94 km (58 miles) wide. It is shaped like a bone, with two knobbly bits at each end.

## Carbonaceous asteroids

C-type, or carbonaceous asteroids, are the most common type. Three-quarters of all asteroids are C-type. They are very dark, as they have lots of carbon and tar in them. The two moons of Mars – Phobos and Deimos – are carbonaceous. Scientists think that these were once asteroids, but then they were captured by the pull of Mars' gravity.

## Shape

Most asteroids are too far away to see clearly, but they seem to come in all sorts of shapes and sizes. Some, like Toutatis, look like knobbly potatoes. Others are smoother and more like spheres.

# Observing asteroids from Earth

Today, astronomers all over the world are working together to create a catalogue of all the asteroids or minor planets. The Minor Planet Centre in Cambridge, USA, keeps the catalogue up-to-date. Details about the asteroids come from all sorts of telescopes – from the Hubble Space Telescope, from huge telescopes in Hawaii, and also from small telescopes in people's back gardens.

## Discovering asteroids

New asteroids are being discovered all the time – and you could be one of the people that finds one. Lots of asteroids are found by amateur astronomers – people who enjoy astronomy as a hobby. To find a new asteroid, astronomers have to take pictures of the night sky using a telescope that has a camera attached. They take a picture of the same piece of sky at different times. They then compare the images and look for an object that has moved. An asteroid looks like a star, while the planets look like round disks.

To find an asteroid, astronomers compare pictures of the night sky, trying to spot a faint star that has moved.

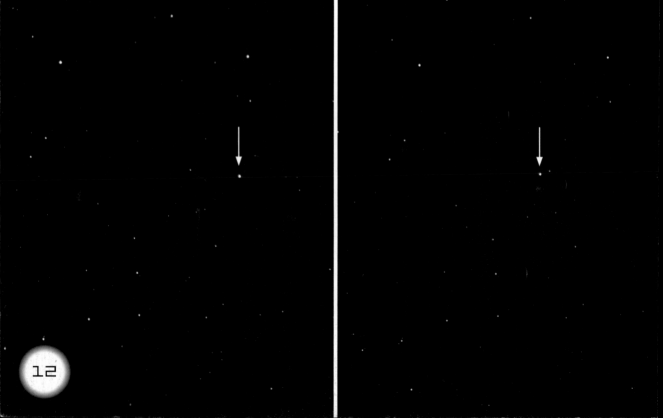

## Working out the shape of an asteroid

Asteroids are strange shapes and they rotate, sometimes in just a few hours. To us they all look like dots in the sky. Depending on the surface and the shape of the asteroid, it will reflect different amounts of light from the Sun. By measuring this light, astronomers can work out its shape and how long it takes to rotate.

### TRY IT YOURSELF:
**See an asteroid**

We can see asteroids because they reflect light from the Sun, as planets do. However, they are smaller than planets and far away, so they don't shine very brightly in the sky. The only asteroid that can be seen with the naked eye is Vesta, and even that is very difficult to see. Vesta, Pallas and Juno are the easiest asteroids to look for.

To see an asteroid, you will need a telescope or good pair of binoculars. You will be looking for a "star" that is not normally there, so having a good map of the stars will help. Charts to help you find the minor planets are published in astronomy magazines or on the Internet (for instance at http://www.heavens-above.com). Watch the asteroid over several nights, and you should be able to see that it has moved against the background of stars.

Asteroids are so far away that it is difficult to take clear pictures of them. You can just make out the shape and craters on this one.

# Visiting asteroids

The first spacecraft to visit an asteroid was the **space probe** *Galileo* (named in honour of the great Italian scientist Galileo Galilei, 1564–1642). *Galileo* actually passed two asteroids, Gaspra (1991) and Ida (1993). It got really close to Gaspra and discovered that the asteroid is 15 km (9 miles) across. Ida is much larger; it is 56 km (35 miles) long. *Galileo* even found a small moon orbiting around Ida, which was named Dactyl. Scientists have worked out that Ida has lots of holes inside it.

Very few spacecraft have visited asteroids, so this is a very special picture of Ida.

## SCIENCE FACT OR SCIENCE FICTION? Mining asteroids

The science fiction writer Isaac Asimov wrote a book called *I, Robot*, which was a series of short stories about robots. In one story, robots mine asteroids for precious metals. Could we really get precious metals from asteroids? Eros, for example, probably contains over 20,000 tonnes of aluminium, gold, and platinum. This is more than has been mined on Earth. Scientists think that it should be possible to mine asteroids. Energy from the Sun could be used to power spacecraft and the machinery. And robots could be used to do the actual mining.

### NEAR-Shoemaker visits Eros

In 2000 another spacecraft, called NEAR-Shoemaker, reached the asteroid Eros. Eros is fairly near to Earth (195 million km, 120 million miles). It is an oblong shape, 33 km (20 miles) by 13 km (8 miles). NEAR-Shoemaker orbited Eros for about a year and took over 160,000 pictures of the asteroid. From these images, scientists identified 100,000 craters and about a million boulders bigger than houses. Then, in February 2001, scientists decided to land NEAR on Eros. The spacecraft sent back 69 more images as it landed, but it was damaged during the landing and stopped transmitting.

### Bringing asteroid samples back to Earth

*Hayabusa* is a Japanese spacecraft that is designed to bring back samples of material from an asteroid. This should help scientists find out more about how the Solar System was formed. *Hayabusa* was launched in 2003 and is due back to Earth in 2007. The asteroid it will visit is 480 million km (300 million miles) from Earth.

NEAR-Shoemaker was the first spacecraft to land on an asteroid, and it wasn't even designed to do that!

# Will an asteroid hit Earth?

Asteroids, comets, and meteoroids have hit the Earth in the past. So we can be sure that an asteroid will hit Earth at some point in the future. The big question is – when? Scientists estimate that very large impacts that affect the whole Earth happen about once every 100,000 years. Smaller impacts affecting a country or an ocean happen more often, about once every century.

## How close is close?

There are over 3500 known near-Earth asteroids, about 790 of which are over a kilometre wide. These asteroids travel across Earth's orbit. One day, one of these asteroids could crash into us.

Astronomers are watching the near-Earth asteroids and working out their exact routes across space. However, with so many asteroids, this takes a long time. It is difficult to work out the orbit of an asteroid accurately. Astronomers have to make many observations. So far, they haven't discovered an asteroid that is likely to hit the Earth.

This is an artist's impression of how the Chicxulub crater was formed. This event may have caused the extinction of the dinosaurs.

In 1908, 60 million trees were flattened when an asteroid exploded above Tunguska in Siberia. You can still see them today.

## SCIENCE FACT OR SCIENCE FICTION: What killed the dinosaurs?

Did an asteroid impact kill off the dinosaurs? A large asteroid impact could cause huge wildfires, **tsunamis**, and volcanic activity. These could reduce the amount of sunlight on Earth for many years. Fewer plants would grow, and animals would have less to eat. So it is possible that an asteroid impact could have caused the death of the dinosaurs. There is evidence that a large asteroid did hit the Earth 65 million years ago (about when the dinosaurs died out). A huge crater has been found that was formed at that time. But not all scientists agree that this was what caused the dinosaur extinction.

## What will happen if we do get hit?

If an asteroid does hit the Earth, what will happen? A large object exploded above Tunguska in Russia in 1908. Scientists at the time thought that it was a comet or an asteroid, but they were not sure which. In 2001, Italian scientists reported the results of a long study of the explosion. They think that it was an asteroid about 60 metres (200 feet) across, exploding 5–8 km (3–5 miles) above the Earth. It had the same energy as about 1000 atom bombs. The explosion flattened 2150 square km (830 square miles) of Siberia. If this had happened over a large city, hundreds of thousands of people would have died.

# What is a comet?

Every few years, a bright tail of light appears in the skies over Earth. It stays there for days, slowly moving across the sky. If you see something like this, it is probably a comet. The name comet comes from the Greek word *kometes*, meaning long-haired.

## A dirty snowball

A comet is sometimes called a dirty snowball or a dirty iceberg. Comets are giant lumps of ice and rock that orbit around the Sun. They spend most of their time in cold regions of space far from the Sun.

In the middle of a comet is the **nucleus**. This is a hard lump of ice and **carbon dioxide ice**, small grains of stone and dust. The nucleus of a comet is normally about 1 to 10 km (0.6 to 6 miles) long.

This is an artist's idea of what the surface of a comet might look like, with craters and huge lumps of ice.

## Melting ice

The nucleus of a comet is too small to be seen from Earth. But sometimes a comet's orbit brings it closer to the Sun. When this happens, the outer part of the snowball starts to melt. As the ice warms up, it becomes a cloud of gas surrounding the nucleus. The gas cloud is called a **coma**. It reflects light from the Sun, and makes the comet more visible.

## Wispy tails

Not all the material that melts stays close to the nucleus. Some stretches away from the nucleus in two very long, wispy tails. These can stretch for millions of kilometres into space. If the comet is close enough to Earth, they can usually be seen without binoculars. One tail is called a dust tail and is made from small particles, the size of smoke particles. The dust tails look yellow. The second tail is a plasma tail and looks blue. The plasma tail is made of electrically charged gases.

A comet's tail is the biggest thing you can see in the night sky. They can stretch for millions of kilometres.

## TRY IT YOURSELF:

Have a go at making your own comet nucleus. Make a snowball, or collect some ice from the freezer and crush it. In a plastic bag, mix the crushed ice with a handful of dirt, a few drops of Worcester sauce or tomato sauce and some fine gravel or sand. Squash the contents into a ball. Put the plastic bag into the freezer and leave it for a couple of hours until it is really hard. The ice is the frozen water found on comets, the sand or gravel is the stony material, as is the dirt, which will make it black. The Worcester sauce represents the carbon-based materials scientists find in comets.

# Where do comets come from?

Comets were probably formed at the same time as the Solar System. There are two kinds of comets, long-period comets and short-period comets.

## The Oort cloud comets

Most long-period comets come from a place in the Solar System called the Oort cloud. The Oort cloud surrounds the Solar System. It is a very long way away, stretching out to about 5 trillion km (3 trillion miles) from the Sun. The comets in the Oort cloud are not just a long way from the Sun – they are also millions of kilometres away from each other.

## How were they made?

When the Solar System was forming, most of the material that formed was much closer to the Sun. Scientists think that the Oort cloud comets were formed in the same region as the giant outer planets. The comets gradually got pushed further away from the Sun by the gravity of the large planets. Eventually they landed up in the Oort cloud. Some may even have left the Solar System altogether.

There are many comets waiting to be discovered in the Oort cloud and the Kuiper belt.

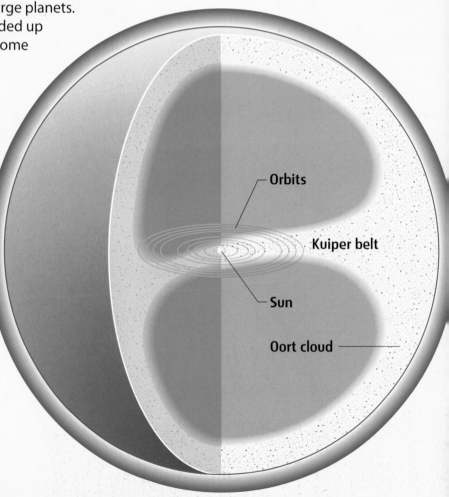

Orbits

Kuiper belt

Sun

Oort cloud

## The Kuiper belt comets

The second group of comets, the short-period comets, come from the Kuiper belt. The Kuiper belt is much closer to the Sun than the Oort cloud. It is out past the orbit of Neptune, between 4.5 and 7.5 billion km (2.8 and 4.7 billion miles) from the Sun. The Kuiper belt is a disc shape and contains lots of small icy objects. There may be as many as 35,000 Kuiper belt objects bigger than 100 km (62 miles) across. Not all the Kuiper belt objects are comets, and some scientists think that Pluto and its moon, Charon, are Kuiper belt objects. The first Kuiper belt object was found in 1992 by astronomers using a telescope in Hawaii.

### BIOGRAPHY:

#### Jan Oort (1900–1992)

Jan Oort was born in the Netherlands and worked at the country's Leiden observatory. He was director of the observatory from 1945 to 1970. In 1950, Oort noticed that comets did not seem to come from outer space. He also found out that comets come from all directions in the sky and that they have huge orbits. He proposed that they came from a cloud surrounding the Solar System. This is now called the Oort cloud.

Jan Oort did not live to see any proof of the existence of the Oort cloud. Even today, astronomers don't have complete proof of its existence.

# What happens to comets?

Comets travel in a path around the Sun. There are two main kinds of path. Some comets move in periodic orbits. This means that they keep coming back to the same place, just like the planets. Scientists think that other comets move along **parabolic** paths. These comets travel in towards the Sun, swinging around and moving off in a different direction. They will never come back.

The comets moving in periodic orbits can take hundreds or even millions of years to travel once around the Sun. However, some take much less time than this. Comet Encke, for instance, only takes three and a half years to go around the Sun.

Planets orbit the Sun along paths that are nearly circles. Comets move in orbits much less circular than the orbits of the planets. They are long, stretched ellipses.

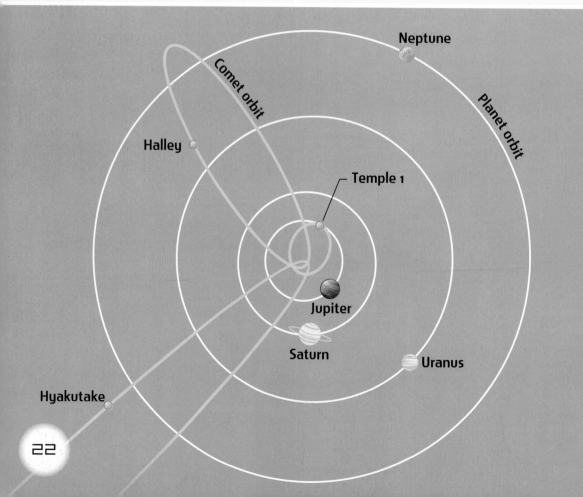

## Comet orbits

Sometimes, the strong gravity of the large planets changes the orbit of a comet. Halley's comet came too close to Jupiter on a long-period orbit or a parabolic path. Jupiter's gravity pulled at the comet and changed it into a shorter periodic comet. Comet Halley now takes 76 years to orbit the Sun. Gravity can also change a comet's orbit to send it completely out of the Solar System.

## Disappearing comets

Every time a comet gets close to the Sun, some of its icy nucleus turns to gas and dust. The comet can eventually disappear, leaving just a cloud of dust and gas behind it. Some comets crash into planets or moons. In 1994, Comet Shoemaker-Levy 9 crashed into Jupiter. The crash was spectacular because the comet had split into lots of pieces before it hit Jupiter.

When Comet Shoemaker-Levy crashed into Jupiter, the bigger pieces caused massive explosions. These left scars in the planet's cloud.

## BIOGRAPHY:
### Edmond Halley (1656–1742)

Edmond Halley went to Oxford University, but he did not finish his degree. Instead, he did lots of astronomy, mapping the stars in the southern hemisphere.

Halley was the first to realize that comets can travel in orbits. In 1705 he published a book showing that a comet seen in 1682 had the same orbit as comets seen by different people over several hundred years. They were actually seeing the same comet returning again and again. The comet was named Halley's comet in his honour.

# Water on comets

Comets often contain frozen water and frozen gases of the sort that are now found in the atmospheres of the inner planets. Could there be a connection between comets and the water and gases on planets?

## No air or water

When the Solar System formed billions of years ago, the planets were extremely hot. Any water or atmospheric gases would have been lost into space. The Earth at this time would not have had any air or water.

Shortly after they were formed, the planets were bombarded with many asteroids and comets. These comets would have contained frozen gases that would have been released on impact. Some scientists think that these gases could have been the source of the atmospheres of the rocky planets (Mercury, Venus, Earth, and Mars). However, other scientists disagree with this theory.

When comets get close to the planets, they can break up into smaller fragments. In 2001 Comet LINEAR broke up in this way. Scientists studying the break-up discovered that LINEAR's water was similar to that on Earth.

University of Hawaii

**Hubble Space Telescope**
WFPC2

## HOT NEWS:

In 2001, scientists in the USA tested the idea that comets could bring life to Earth. They put some of the chemicals needed for life onto a bullet and fired it at high speed onto a target. The chemicals survived the collision. Chemicals like these have been found in meteorites and dust clouds in space.

Fragments of comets have been hitting the planets and moons for a long time. They can create chains of craters on the surface, like these on Jupiter's moon Ganymede.

### Does water on Earth come from comets?

Comets also contain ice, so they might also have brought water to the surface of the planets. About 1 water **molecule** in 3200 found on Earth is slightly heavier than normal. This water contains two extra small particles called neutrons. By measuring how many heavy molecules of water there are in different water samples, scientists can tell if the water came from the same place.

Comet LINEAR was studied in 2000 and its water is quite similar to water on Earth. Some scientists think that comets that formed near to Jupiter probably had similar water to the water found on Earth. However, evidence from Comet Hale Bopp suggests that Earth's water did not come from comets.

### Did comets bring life?

Some scientists suggest that other chemicals needed for life came to Earth on comets. They have already found some signs that these chemicals do exist on comets. To get more evidence, spacecraft will have to visit comets and examine what they are made of. Several spacecraft are already attempting to do this. When they complete their missions, we may find out whether comets really did bring water, and perhaps the other chemicals needed for life, to Earth.

# Comets through history

Comets have amazed and scared people all over the world for many years. Imagine looking up at the sky and seeing a strange streak of light. If you didn't know what it was, you might be worried too. When they saw a comet or large **meteor shower**, people used to predict that the world would end. This is not so far from the truth. If a large comet did hit the Earth, it would cause devastation. But we now know that most comets we see are too far away to be dangerous.

## Comets in different cultures

There are references to fires in the skies in many cultures. They were written about in Babylonia, Persia, China, and in the Bible. In some cultures, people thought that the comet looked like the head of a woman, with long flowing hair. This was a sign of mourning, and meant that the gods were not very happy and something bad would happen. Other people thought that the comet looked like a fiery sword, and this meant that a war was coming. Chinese astronomers kept records of the comets they saw for many years. This record-keeping has been very useful to later scientists, who have been able to learn a lot about comet movements from them.

This engraving shows a comet that appeared over Augsburg, Germany, in November 1618. At that time, comets were often regarded as bad omens.

Halley's comet has appeared every 76 years for over 2000 years. We are next due to see it in 2062.

**Watch out for a comet**

There are 168 named periodic comets, such as Halley's comet. Depending on their brightness, they can be seen with the naked eye, binoculars or a telescope. Although comets are always visible from Earth, most are very faint and are hard to see. "Great" comets with long tails, which are easy to see with the naked eye, don't come along very often and are usually unexpected. On average, one appears every 5-10 years. It's best to check the Internet to find out when and where comets are visible.

## Halley's comet

The comet that Edmond Halley described in 1705 is one of the most famous comets in history. It can be seen from Earth every 76 years, so plenty of people have had the chance to see it. The earliest record of Halley's comet is from China in 240BC, over 2000 years ago. The comet also appeared just before the Norman Conquest of England in 1066. People thought that the comet was a bad omen for England's King Harold, and in fact he died in the Battle of Hastings later that year.

# Looking at comets

Very few comets have been visited by spacecraft. This is not surprising, as they are normally so far away. The most visited comet is Halley's Comet . The space probe *Giotto* visited Halley's comet in 1986, as did four other spacecraft from all over the world. *Giotto* also visited a comet called Grigg-Skjellerup.

## Collecting stardust

*Stardust* is a spacecraft sent by **NASA** to Comet Wild 2. This comet probably formed near Pluto, right at the edge of the Solar System. It has only recently come close enough for us to visit it. The mission reached Comet Wild 2 in January 2004 and *Stardust* flew within 240 km (149 miles) of its nucleus. It collected thousands of dust particles from the comet and is due back on Earth in 2006. It will land in the Great Salt Lake desert early in the morning. Scientists are hopeful that the dust will give them new information about the origins of the Solar System, or even the origin of life on Earth.

This is a photograph of comet Shoemaker-Levy 9 orbiting Jupiter. It has split into several pieces. Some of the pieces hit Jupiter in 1994.

## HOT NEWS:
### A Wild comet

Comet Wild 2 is nothing like scientists expected. The photos from the *Stardust* spacecraft show that there are steep cliffs, tall pinnacles, high, flat areas and craters on its surface. Scientists were expecting to find that dust left the comet in one jet. However, they found dozens of small regions pushing dust out into space. When *Stardust* flew past the comet, it was hit by bursts of dust with quiet breaks in between each burst.

## Landing on a comet

*Rosetta* is a spacecraft that was launched by the European Space Agency on 2 March 2004. *Rosetta* is travelling to Comet 67 P/ Churyumov-Gerasimenko. The spacecraft has a very long journey ahead of it – over 800 million km (480 million miles). It will not reach the comet until 2014. When *Rosetta* does arrive, it will orbit the comet. The spacecraft will examine the comet as it comes nearer to the Sun, looking at the way the tail and coma are formed. *Rosetta* will also try and land on the comet. A tiny probe called *Philae* will attach itself to the comet's nucleus.

This is a computer simulation of *Stardust's* sample return capsule arriving back on Earth in 2006.

# Deep Impact

*Deep Impact* is a NASA mission to look inside the middle of a comet. The probe visited Comet Tempel 1 in 2005. Comet Tempel 1 a periodic comet that takes about 5.5 years to orbit the Sun. Its nucleus is estimated to be 14 km (9 miles) long, and 4.5 km (3 miles) wide. The comet is visible from Earth using a large telescope. Fortunately, *Deep Impact* got close enough to take some good photos of the comet.

## Making a crater on a comet

The *Deep Impact* spacecraft was launched on 12 January 2005 and reached Tempel 1 later that year. The comet was 130 million km (80 million miles) from Earth. As it got close, the main spacecraft released a small impactor spacecraft on a collision course with the comet. On 4 July 2005  the impactor crashed into the comet at 14,000 km/h (23,000 mph), making a hole perhaps 200 metres (650 feet) across. The main *Deep Impact* spacecraft recorded the effects of the collision. Telescopes on Earth and in space also watched as the collision took place.

*Deep Impact* ready for launch at Cape Canaveral Air Force Station, Florida, USA in January 2005.

When the impactor hit the comet, there was a large flash of light, and clouds of material were thrown off the surface of the comet. Scientists are analysing the huge amount of data that was gathered during the impact. They hope that their results will give us information about the difference between the inside and the outside of the comet.

## SCIENCE FACT OR SCIENCE FICTION?

In the film *Deep Impact*, a comet is discovered to be heading towards the Earth. It is so big that a crash could mean the end of the human race. Politicians must decide what to do to save us. Astronauts are sent to deflect the incoming comet from the Earth using nuclear weapons.

Scientists expect a large comet to hit the Earth one day, but it probably won't happen for a very long time. They are not sure how we would try and stop it reaching Earth. If they did decide to explode the comet, the smaller bits would probably still hit the Earth. One idea would be to move the comet away from Earth's orbit, but no-one is quite sure how we could do that.

Would a comet impact look like this scene from the film *Deep Impact*?

# Meteoroids, meteorites, and meteors

Meteoroids are small fragments of rock or metal, drifting through space. They come from asteroids, planets, moons, or the dust tail of a comet. Most meteoroids are very small – they are no more than pieces of dust. However some are much bigger. The biggest meteoroids are 100 metres (330 feet) across. There isn't really a clear difference between asteroids and meteoroids. Some people think of meteoroids as space rocks approaching the Earth.

## Burning up in the atmosphere

If meteoroids come close enough to Earth, they crash through the atmosphere. When this happens, they burn up. If it is dark, you can see the streaks of light they make in the sky. We call these streaks meteors or shooting stars. If the meteoroid is big enough it can explode and become something called a fireball. Scientists estimate that millions of meteoroids reach Earth and burn up in the atmosphere every day.

When they enter the atmosphere, meteoroids are travelling very fast. Friction with the atmosphere can make them red-hot.

This is a crater in the window of the Space Shuttle *Challenger*, possibly caused by the impact of a tiny meteoroid. The picture has been magnified by 100 times.

## HOW IT WORKS: High friction

Why do meteoroids burn up in the atmosphere? The answer is friction. Meteoroids hit the top of the atmosphere at high speed, between 16 and 64 km (10 and 40 miles) per second. The atmosphere is made of different gases, and friction between the meteoroid and these gases slows the meteoroid down. Friction also makes the meteoroid very hot. You can feel how friction heats things up by rubbing your palms together for a minute. At the end of the minute they will feel very warm.

## Crashing to the ground

If a meteoroid is bigger than a marble, it won't completely burn up in the atmosphere. Part of it will crash into the ground. A meteoroid the size of a football can explode on the way down. Any meteoroid that actually hits the Earth is called a meteorite.

Some meteorites fall through the atmosphere at such a speed that the outside gets hot enough to melt. These meteorites have a black crust on the outside. Once it reaches the ground, the crust can start to go rusty and turn orangey brown. Most of the meteorites we find on the ground are quite small. They are so light that they slowed down quickly and were not melted as they fell through the atmosphere.

# Shooting stars

There is a lot of dust floating around in space. As the Earth moves through space, it sweeps up the dust, a bit like you would if you walked past a bonfire. The dust particles crash down into Earth's atmosphere. They move so fast that they burn up in the atmosphere and leave a streak of light behind them. The streak of light is called a meteor or shooting star. Meteor means "something in the air".

You can look for meteors on any clear night, but you are more likely to see them at certain times of the year. They are best seen with the naked eye rather than a telescope.

## Dust in space

Where does all the dust in space come from? As a comet moves through space, it leaves a trail of dust and ice behind it. Meteor showers happen when the Earth passes through this trail. Not all meteors come from comets. Some of the dust is left over from the formation of the Solar System. There is even a lot of space junk (bits that have fallen off satellites and spacecraft) that can crash into the Earth's atmosphere, leaving a streak of light behind it.

## TRY IT YOURSELF:
### Meteor watching

Random or sporadic meteors can be seen every night. They appear on average every 10 minutes. In an hour, you could see six meteors. You can't predict what direction they will come from though. Choose a clear night with a new Moon, as it will be darker and you are more likely to see meteors. It is best to lie down in a place where you can see as much of the sky as possible. Make sure you wear lots of warm clothes, a hat and some gloves if it is a cold night.

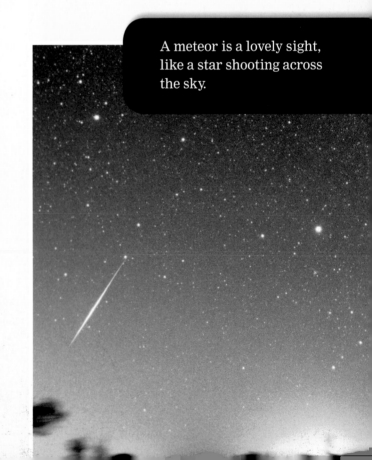

A meteor is a lovely sight, like a star shooting across the sky.

## Fireballs

Fireballs are very bright meteors. They are so bright that if you were outside when one happened, you would see it even if you weren't looking for it. Sometimes fireballs are so bright that they can be seen in the day time and occasionally you might even hear an explosion. It is more common to see them at sunset. Most people only see one in their lifetime, but the more you look, the more you are likely to see!

Fireballs are quite rare, but if one happened near to you, you would not be able to miss it!

# Meteor showers

Meteor showers can be spectacular to watch. Instead of seeing five or six meteors an hour, you will see tens of meteors every hour. You could even see hundreds of them if you are very lucky. In a meteor shower, many streaks of light appear across the sky, like fiery rain. If you leave the shutter on a camera open for a few minutes, you might even capture them on film. Meteor showers happen when the Earth passes through a trail of dust left by a comet.

## Looking along the path of a comet

If you watch a meteor shower, you might notice that the meteors all appear to come from the same point in the sky. This point is called the **radiant**. The meteor shower is named after the constellation where the radiant is. Although the meteors will all seem to go in different directions from this point, they are actually travelling in lines along the path of a comet. They appear to come to a point because of perspective. This is just like looking at long, straight railway tracks that seem to meet in the distance.

### TRY IT YOURSELF:
**Catch a meteor shower**

The Leonids appear in November. They are at their most spectacular around 17–18 November. The Perseids are a summer meteor shower. They are best seen around 12 August. Some people have been very lucky, and witnessed one of the great meteor showers, with tens of streaks of light crossing the sky,

Artists have often created pictures of meteor showers to record the event.

### The Leonids

The most spectacular meteor shower seen in the last century was early in the morning on 17 November 1966. It was a Leonid meteor shower. Over 50 meteors were seen every second. Leonid showers happen every year. The Leonids are caused by Comet Tempel-Tuttle, which was discovered by Ernst Tempel and Horace Tuttle in 1866. Comet Tempel-Tuttle has a 33-year orbit around the Sun, and so Earth passes through a thicker part of the comet's trail about every 33 years. There are lots more meteors when this happens. The earliest recorded sighting of the Leonids was in AD 902. The meteoroids travel at about 257,000 km (159,000 miles) per hour. They are very small, about the size of a grain of sand.

### The Perseids

In 1837, Edward Herrick was the first person to realize that there was a meteor shower every August. He had spotted a now famous meteor shower called the Perseids. They were associated with Comet Swift-Tuttle.

# Space rocks

If a meteor doesn't burn up completely, it will eventually fall to the ground. It is then called a meteorite. Scientists estimate that about 300,000 meteorites fall to the ground every year, although a lot of these fall into the oceans. Most of these meteorites are small: only about a thousand of them are bigger than a football. The largest meteorite ever found weighs 60 tonnes. It is about 3 metres (10 feet) square and 1 metre (3 feet) high and was found in Hoba in Namibia.

## Falls and finds

Scientists sort meteorites into falls and finds. Falls are meteorites found by someone who saw it land or worked out that one had landed there. A meteorite is called a find if it has been collected by someone who has no idea of when it fell to Earth.

Iron meteorites look so different from normal rocks that you are not likely to mistake them for something from Earth.

## Irons

Some meteorites contain iron – they are called irons. Most finds are irons because they are so different from normal rocks that they are quite easy to identify. Irons are attracted to magnets, and this also makes them easier to find. However, only 5 per cent of falls are irons. This shows that in fact this kind of meteorite is quite rare.

## Stony meteorites

There are lots of other kinds of meteorites. Chondrites are stony meteorites that have not been melted since they originally formed, soon after the Solar System began. Achondrites are stony meteorites that have melted at some point in the past. There are also stony-iron meteorites, which are half stone and half metal. Not all meteorites come from comets or space dust. There are also some lunar meteorites (currently 31 have been found) and some Martian meteorites (currently 37).

The inside of a meteorite looks quite different to the outside.

# Meteorite hunting

Anyone can find a meteorite – you don't have to be an astronomer or a scientist! Meteorites can fall to the ground anywhere. There could be a meteorite in your garden or a nearby field, on a beach or in a wood. You need to work out whether the rocks you pick up are normal rocks or meteorites.

All meteorites will feel heavier than normal rock, but some kinds are easier to spot than others. It is easier to spot metal meteorites, as they aren't like normal rocks. They are mainly made of iron, which is very different from the other rocks you might find.

## In Antarctica

The Antarctic is a good place to look for meteorites. This is not because more meteorites fall here, but because they are easier to find as they collect in some areas and are easy to spot against the white ice. The first Antarctic meteorite was found in 1912. A team of scientists visits the Antarctic every year to hunt for meteorites. They find hundreds on each trip.

Meteorites that fall in Antarctica move with the flow of the ice. In places where the ice runs into an obstacle it is worn away, leaving behind the meteorites.

## In the desert

Deserts are another good place to look, as they normally don't have many rocks. New meteorites will look black, as they still have the burnt crust they got when coming through the atmosphere. As they are black, they stand out well against the desert background.

## What will we find out?

Meteorites come from all over the Solar System. They are very useful as they give us a way of exploring space without leaving Earth. Scientists study meteorites to find out about how the Earth and the rest of the Solar System formed. They also want to know about the different materials that make up the Solar System, and where they might have come from.

### TRY IT YOURSELF:
**Find a meteorite**

The best place for anyone to look for a meteorite is somewhere meteorites have already been found. You could look in your library to see if anyone has ever found a meteorite near you. Tape a strong magnet to the bottom of a stick (a walking stick or golf club would work well). Push the stick in and out of the undergrowth and near any rocks. Iron meteorites will be attracted to your stick. Remember to get permission from the landowner before hunting for meteorites.

Anyone can search for meteorites, even you!

Scientists don't know when the Earth will next get hit by a large asteroid or comet. They have estimated that roughly every 100,000 years there is a crash large enough to affect the whole Earth. Smaller impacts happen more frequently. Something on the scale of the impact in Tunguska in Russia (see page 17) happens about once every century.

### Will it make a big crater?
If the Earth does get hit, what would happen? Well, it depends on the size of the object that hits us and where and how it lands. A smaller object that explodes in the atmosphere, like the one at Tunguska in Russia, would flatten an area. The impact might also start fires. If an object lands in the ocean, it could create a tsunami. This would damage the coastline around the ocean. If an object reaches land, it would create a crater, like those we see on Mars or the Moon.

A really large object could cause a lot of damage. It could cause an earthquake or activate some volcanoes. A lot of dust and debris would rise into the air, and could cover the Sun for a time.

An asteroid could hit the Earth
anywhere, on land or in the sea.

## Watching out for space rocks

Because scientists expect the Earth to get hit at some point, they are now getting prepared. There are monitoring stations working out the orbits of as many asteroids and comets as possible. By doing this, scientists should be able to provide us with some warning of a crash, and maybe even give us a few hundred years to plan what to do. Governments are also starting to think about how they could prevent any collision. It is most likely that they would try to change the comet or asteroid's orbit, so that it would miss the Earth completely. They would be unlikely to blow it up, as this would probably mean lots of smaller asteroids hitting the Earth instead.

### HOW IT WORKS:
**The Near Earth Object Program**

NASA's Near Earth Object Program is detecting and tracking potentially dangerous objects. It is attempting to locate about 90 per cent of the estimated 1000 large objects (bigger than 1 km, 0.6 mile) that could crash into Earth. About 3500 near-Earth objects have been discovered so far, and about 790 of these are larger than 1 km (0.6 mile). NASA have classified just over 700 of these as possibly dangerous.

When a volcano erupts, it sends a lot of fine ash high into the air. Some of this ash travels around the world. If enough volcanoes erupted, they could darken the sky across the globe.

# How to watch meteor showers

## Meteor showers

If you want to watch a meteor shower, choose a dark clear night and wrap up warm.
Find yourself a sun-lounger. Position yourself so you have a good view of the sky,
away from streetlamps and as far from buildings as possible.

| Meteor shower | When to watch | The peak | Where to watch |
|---|---|---|---|
| Perseids | 23 July–22 August | 12 August | northern hemisphere |
| Orionids | 15–29 October | 21 October | northern and southern hemisphere |
| Leonids | 13–20 November | 17 November | northern and southern hemisphere |
| Geminids | 6–19 December | 14 December | northern and southern hemisphere |

## The major asteroids

Visit http://www.heavens-above.com to find out when you can see these asteroids.

| Asteroid | Mean distance from Sun | Diameter of largest axis | Date discovered | Discoverer |
|---|---|---|---|---|
| Ceres (now a dwarf planet) | 414 million km (257 million miles) | 960 km (597 miles) | 1801 | Giuseppe Piazzi |
| Pallas | 415 million km (258 milllion miles) | 570 km (354 miles) | 1802 | Heinrich Olbers |
| Juno | 399 million km (248 million miles) | 240 km (249 miles) | 1804 | Karl Harding |
| Vesta | 353 million km (219 million miles) | 530 km (329 miles) | 1807 | Heinrich Olbers |

## Near Earth comets

This table shows the comets that will be closer to Earth than one-tenth of the average distance between the Sun and the Earth between 2005 and 2020. Astronomers do not yet know how bright they will be when they approach the Earth.

| Comet | Date of closest approach to Earth | Distance from Earth |
|---|---|---|
| 73P/Schwassmann-Wachmann-C | 12 May 2006 | 11.4 million km (7.1 million miles) |
| 45P/Honda-Mrkos-Pajdusakova | 15 August 2011 | 9 million km (5.6 million miles) |
| P/2004 CB (LINEAR) | 28 May 2014 | 7.5 million km (4.7 million miles) |
| P/2000 G1 (LINEAR) | 22 March 2016 | 4.9 million km (3 million miles) |
| 45P/Honda-Mrkos-Pajdusakova | 11 February 2017 | 13 million km (8.1 million miles) |
| 46P/Wirtanen | 16 December 2018 | 11.6 million km (7.2 million miles) |

# Glossary

**asteroid** minor planet orbiting the Sun

**asteroid belt** the region between the orbits of Mars and Jupiter that contains many millions of asteroids. Also known as the "main belt".

**atmosphere** gas held by gravity around a Solar System body

**carbon dioxide ice** frozen carbon dioxide

**coma** cloud of gas found around a comet's nucleus

**comet** large block of ice, rock, and dust that orbits the Sun

**core** the innermost region of a planet or moon, usually made of nickel and iron

**crater** hole caused by the impact of a comet or meteorite

**dwarf planet** small body in the solar system which is not large enough to be called a planet

**ellipse** regular oval shape

**gravity** force that pulls objects together

**matter** physical material. Solids, liquids, and gases are all forms of matter.

**meteor** a meteoroid that entered the Earth's atmosphere and burnt up. Also known as a shooting star.

**meteor shower** flurry of meteors at a particular time of the year that seem to come from the same point

**meteorite** meteoroid that entered the Earth's atmosphere and reached the surface

**meteoroids** small fragments of rock or metal that may be pieces of planets, moons, comets or asteroids

**molecule** two or more atoms joined together

**moon** a rocky body that orbits a planet

**NASA** the National Aeronautics and Space Administration, the United States space agency

**nucleus** the innermost part of something, for instance a comet

**orbit** the path of an astronomical object moving around another

**parabolic** in the shape of a parabola, which is the curved shape of the flight of an object that has been thrown

**planet** a large body of rock or gas that orbits the Sun or another star

**radar** device used to locate objects that cannot be seen

**radiant** the point in the sky where meteors in a meteor shower appear to come from

**radio telescope** a scientific instrument that can detect radio waves from space

**Solar System** the planets and their moons, asteroids, comets, meteoroids, etc. that orbit around the Sun

**space probe** a spacecraft with scientific instruments designed to examine a Solar System body

**tsunami** a huge wave generated when a large volume of the sea is displaced suddenly, for instance after a large undersea earthquake or the impact of a large meteorite

# Further information

Couper, Heather and Henbest, Nigel. *Encyclopedia of Space* (Dorling Kindersley, 2003).

Henbest, Nigel. *The Night Sky* (Usborne, 2000).

Poskitt, Kjartan. *The Gobsmacking Galaxy* (Scholastic, 2004).

Prinja, Raman. *Visions of the Universe: The Latest Discoveries in Space Reveale*d (Mitchell Beazley, 2004).

## Places to visit

**Royal Observatory**
Greenwich
London
SE10 9NF
UK
+44 (0)20 8312 6565
www.rog.nmm.ac.uk/

**Siding Spring Observatory**
Coonabarabran
National Park Road
New South Wales
Australia
+64 (0)2 68-426211
www.sidingspringexploratory.com.au

## Websites

**Windows to the Universe: history and people**
*http://www.windows.ucar.edu/tour/link=/people/people.html*
A user-friendly guide to the Earth and space science. There are easy, intermediate, and advanced versions of each article, so you can choose the level you want to read at.

**The brief history of astronomy**
*http://www.geocities.com/CapeCanaveral/1612/history.html*
This website has not been updated for 10 years, but it still gives a good overview of the history of astronomy.

**Space and beyond** *http://kids.msfc.nasa.gov/Space/*
A website about stars, black holes, quasars, and other space stuff, from NASA. Also includes Astronomy Picture of the Day.

# Index